Wedding dress shopping

A guide for every bride to be

Written by E E Dorothy

Illustrated by Kathryn Francis

Dedication

To my girls

My world and my why

Table of Contents

Acknowledgments

To my family, for always being there.

Introduction

Congratulations on your engagement!

After the celebrations the planning begins! But where to start!? Choosing your wedding dress is top of the list. It will be the most difficult decision as well as the most expensive purchase of clothing you will ever make. Yet at the same time it will be a enjoyable and memorable experience.

Working in the bridal industry and helping many brides find their perfect dress I have gathered together the most important tips to help you on your journey to finding the one.

Every brides journey to finding the one is different but I hope these helpful tips can make that journey more enjoyable and the experience of bridal dress shopping even more memorable for you.

So let's begin!

The Venue

The Venue

Choose your venue and secure your date! Securing your date and location will play a big part in determining what style of dress you will be choosing for your big day. Whether you are getting married in a field, barn, in the winter or spring, having the date and location secured will make saying yes to the dress that bit easier.

When to start looking

When To Start Looking

ridal dresses normally take 3 to 9 months to arrive in to store and then you will need a further 8 to 12 weeks for alterations to be carried out before the big day. Majority of wedding dresses are not made to measure.

You can get dresses made in as little as 3 months but there is normally a rush fee starting from £100 and this doesn't really give any breathing space if any hiccups should appear within this time frame. To avoid such a stressful wait I would strongly recommend ordering a minimum of 12 months before the wedding date.

It is very rare dresses arrive with faults as they are checked before being sent to the store and also rechecked by the store themselves but unfortunately some faults only appear once the bride has put the dress on during her final appointment. By ordering early you will have time to send the dress back for any adjustments and see your chosen seamstresses without the worry of a tight time frame to work with.

12 months is the time to start looking, however you can look sooner if you are too excited to wait! But be careful to not look too soon as you will only confuse yourself and may miss out on the new collections arriving. Once your deposit has been paid it is non-returnable due to dresses being made to order. Brides who have looked as early as 18 -24 months before their wedding date usually do so to help spread the costs of their bridal dress. Many stores today will allow payment plans that are interest free, just having to secure your dress with a 20-25 percent deposit. This can be very appealing if you are on a strict budget and also to allow you to get a dress you may not have been able to get if you left it later than 12 months before your wedding. Most importantly, once you find the dress ....stop looking!

Price range

Price Range

*G*ood quality dresses will start from £800 and go up to £3500 for the majority of bridal boutiques. You will come across or hear of brides trying dresses on over £6000 but these prices are normally seen in high end boutiques that are normally based in places like London.

It is important that you have a price range in mind and that you let your bridal consultant know from the start what it is and you stick to it. It is tempting when you are in the shop to try on dresses that are out of your price range as you just want to see the dress on but 9 times out of 10 that will be the one you love and the one you will end up having to buy as nothing else compares. DON'T DO IT TO YOURSELF.

If you do not have a price range then lucky you! You will have unlimited choice when looking in your chosen boutique. This may give you more choice and make choosing your perfect dress that little more difficult but it is a good place to be in if you are happy to make choosing your dress that bit more difficult.

Sample dresses however can start from as little as £200! If you are prepared to wait and book in as soon as a sale is announced you can then find a designer dress for the fraction of the price. The difference here is that you will be getting a dress that has been tried on by other brides as it has been a shop sample. Many sample dresses can be found in good condition and you can get the dress dry cleaned once your alterations have been completed. You will need to be ready to purchase the dress you love on the day as once the sample has gone it has gone.

Your theme

Your Theme

Not every bride will have a theme for her wedding day but if you can take the time to decide what feel you want to have, this can really help pin point what style of dress you should be getting. Generally, it will help planning the whole wedding that much easier.

For example, If you are thinking of getting married outside and wanting to have a woodland feel for the décor of the wedding, then maybe a boho look will be what you are after as it fits nicely with everything else. Or you may want to consider a dress that is easier to manage when outdoors such as a A-line dress that has a small or no train at the back.

If you have no idea what look you will be having for the big day, then finding you dress first can help you determine this. This is a good way to go about finding your dress as it does not limit you to what styles you should be trying on.

Despite this advice, please remember that it is your wedding day so you ultimately decide what you are wearing, regardless of what you are choosing for your décor.

Bridal boutiques

Bridal Boutiques

Before you got engaged you may have noticed one or two bridal boutiques around or even none! But as soon as you start looking for a dress you are just overwhelmed with so many of them! It won't be long until you know where every bridal boutique is in your area and probably in the surrounding areas as well.

From my experience I would suggest looking at the bridal boutiques in your area first, especially their social media accounts as this can give you an idea of what they are like as a store and most importantly what type of dresses they have. This can immediately give you an idea if you should visit them. Secondly, look at reviews and feedback from others who have already visited. If the majority of feedback is brilliant then you know you will be in good hands. And will have an idea of what to expect when you walk through the door.

Next, I would decide what type of service you want for your bridal shopping experience? If you want a private appointment with a bridal consultant helping you throughout your appointment then an independent bridal boutique is what you should be looking for.

If you are happy to go in and pick out dresses yourself, with no or little advice from the sales consultant and possibly take your chosen dress home with you that day then the big outlet bridal stores is where you should be looking for your dress.

Every bridal boutique is different so before getting in touch I would check their website for more details on how they operate and then start making appointments! It will now start feeling a bit real..........you are getting married!

Book An Appointment

Whether you contact a bridal store by phone, email or drop a message on social media, make sure you have a date when you are free and that the most important people are able to come with you on that day. The majority of brides will find their dress on their first day of shopping and do not be surprised if you become one of those brides as well!

Remember that bridal stores are at their busiest on weekends so expect a fee to be charged in order to book a weekend appointment which is usually around £20. In most cases this is refundable when you arrive for your appointment or if you give plenty of notice of cancelling. If your booking fee is not refundable it usually means you will have a VIP experience when you arrive which may include prosecco and cakes waiting for you and your guests. By researching the bridal boutiques social media and website you will already be aware of this before getting in touch with them.

Once in contact with the store most bridal boutiques will ask a few questions about your wedding such as:

The wedding date,
Where are you getting married?
Where is the reception being held?
Have you tried on dresses before?
Do you have a style in mind for your perfect dress?
Do you have a price range you want to stick to?
Who will be coming with you to your appointment?

This will help them build a picture of what you want for your wedding day and most importantly what you want from your dress and will start helping your bridal consultant to determine what dresses you should be trying with her when you arrive.

Mermaid

Empire

Ball Gown

Short

Fit & Flare

Column

Weekday appointments

Weekday Appointments

Weekday appointments tend to be longer and the store is quieter during your time there. Unless it is half term or the summer break.

Appointments can last for 2 to 2.5 hours depending on how busy the store is that day, compared to weekend appointments which last normally 1 to 1.5 hours.

You will also find you can bring more guests to your appointment if you have a large entourage you really want to be there and sometimes it will also feel like you have the store to yourself…Bonus!

If you can book an appointment during the weekday I would strongly advise this over a weekend appointment as you will have more time and it will make it that little bit easier to decide on the dress for you.

The entourage

The Entourage

Who you bring with you on your hunt for your perfect dress is extremely important. Take some time to think about who will be joining you on your wedding dress shopping experience. They will be helping you find the perfect dress for you so make sure you value their opinion and that they also understand you as well. For example, what they love on you may not be something that you love as it is rather what they would wear themselves.

Unfortunately, I have seen it a number of times where a member of the bridal party has spoilt the appointment for the bride because they are too opiniated or very cutting when the bride has certain dresses on.

With this in mind, majority of bridal boutiques welcome a maximum of 3/4 guests to accompany you to your appointment. This is to help with the above and also to help you to not feel so overwhelmed as too many opinions can cause quite a bit of confusion.

Once you have chosen your entourage, check their availability and get booking! By choosing the most important people to you, they will help make your dress shopping experience plain sailing and help create that memorable experience that you will share always.

What to wear to your appointment

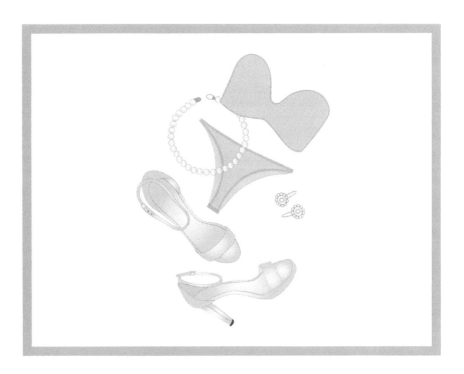

What To Wear
To Your Appointment

To really enjoy your experience and to help visualise exactly what the dress will look like on the big day I would advise wearing and doing the following in preparation for your appointment.

- Nude underwear
- Nude strapless bra
- Minimal makeup
- Shoes with the heel height you expect to wear on the day
- Have your hair done as best you can to what you expect to have it like on the day
- Remove big jewellery and watches unless wanting to wear them on the day

Many bridal shops will have shoes for you to wear but having your own can make sure the heel is correct so gives you an idea of the length for the big day and of course may be more comfortable to wear during your appointment/s.

A strapless bra will make it easier for you to move from dress to dress, however many dresses do not need a bra as they are built in already. So, if you feel comfortable to I would advise wearing no bra throughout your appointment. This is especially helpful if the dress is backless or slightly open in the front.

Remember majority of brides will find their dress on their first day of shopping so it always helps to be as prepared as possible to help visualise exactly what the dress will be like on your big day.

First appointment

First Appointment

*Y*our first appointment will be a bit overwhelming to start with and one that you will always remember. Your bridal consultant will advise to start with a few dresses to begin with that are of different styles and shapes. Once you have tried these all on, you will start to build a picture of what you are wanting from your dress and then your bridal consultant will go back through the collection and pull out the desired dresses.

Even if you think you know what dress you want still start this way to make sure you have not missed anything as the majority of brides will tell you that they picked a dress they never thought they would go for. It happens all the time.

I promise that you will be a professional by the end and you will know exactly what you are doing. Picking out dresses will just start getting easier. Enjoy every minute of trying them on as it will not be long until you find the one.

Bridal sizing

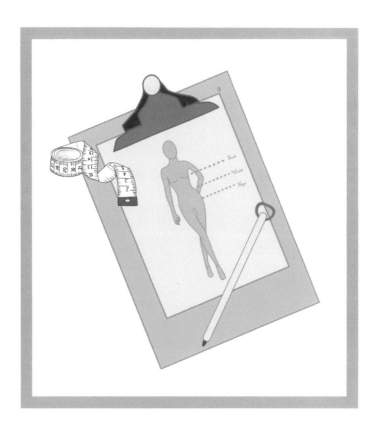

Bridal Sizing

ridal dresses are not sized like the high street stores. On average, expect to jump up to one or two bridal sizes when getting measured for your dress. This is usually because they are sized differently to UK clothing, which is not surprising as many are made abroad, and also because they need to accommodate the corset/boning inside the dress. This needs to be considered as well as the bride's size.

It is just a number and no one will know the size of your dress unless you tell them. As long as it fits properly that is all that matters.

Remember a seamstress can always pull in a dress if it's a little big on you but there is little she can do if the dress is too small. Unless you know that you will drop 2 dress sizes before your dress arrives in store, I would advise ordering the size you are measured as at the time you are ordering your dress.

Majority of dresses can be taking in by 2 dress sizes. Planning a wedding is difficult enough without adding that extra pressure on to yourself.

Listen to your bridal consultant's advice on sizing and get a glass of prosecco in your hand to celebrate finding the one!

Trust your bridal consultant

Bridal Consultant

*T*he moment you meet your bridal consultant it is important you listen to her. It is good to have ideas of what you want, however to find the one, you do need to be open and willing to try different styles on to begin with. The majority of brides will tell you that they chose a dress they never thought they would choose and it was because of their bridal consultant suggesting the dress to be tried during their appointment.

No reputable bridal boutique would train their bridal consultants to put just any dress on a bride and to not advise them on what is best for their shape and style. When you choose your dress and wear it on your wedding day, you will be asked where you got your dress from therefore representing that company. They will always make sure the dress you choose is the perfect dress for you.

Listening to your bridal consultant is again very important when it comes to deciding what size to have! Your bridal consultant knows the dress and how that designer measures up compared to UK sizes. She will have also seen brides who have come to their final appointments and not lost the weight they were adamant they would lose. Don't put this extra pressure on yourself. Enjoy your wedding planning and remember your dress can always be taken in.

Seamstress

Seamstress

*M*ajority of bridal dresses will not be made to measure but rather come in standard sizes. The size chosen will be based on the biggest measurement taken which is usually the hips.

Once your dress has arrived and you have tried it on, the next step is to book a seamstress appointment. The seamstress is the person who will alter your dress to fit you perfectly. Alterations usually take place 8 – 12 weeks before the wedding date. This signals that the wedding is almost here and the count down has begun!.....woohoo!

Some bridal boutiques will have an instore seamstress while others will have recommended seamstresses. The difference is that you will have your alterations at the seamstresses studio and payment made directly to her rather than the bridal boutique you bought the dress from.

A seamstress that is in house or highly recommended by a bridal boutique is done so based on years of experience together and they will remain to work closely together insuring the bride has her perfect dress before the big day.

Please remember that when choosing any seamstress, recommended or not, you must check their reviews and skill level. There will be a few who can alter dresses but have no experience with wedding dresses and can cause more stress to you the bride than there needs to be. If in doubt let your bridal boutique know and they will be happy to help.

Expect to have 2 to 3 fittings before the big day and to make it a smoother process make sure you are happy with your size before your first fitting in order to reduce fluctuating in size and increasing fitting appointments. This is easier said than done!

Budget around £250 for alterations as a ball mark figure. They can however range from £200 to £400 depending on how much altering is needed.

Do not forget to take your wedding shoes, wedding underwear and most trusted person with you to your fittings. Enjoy your time together and of course being back in your dress!

Sample sale or to order new

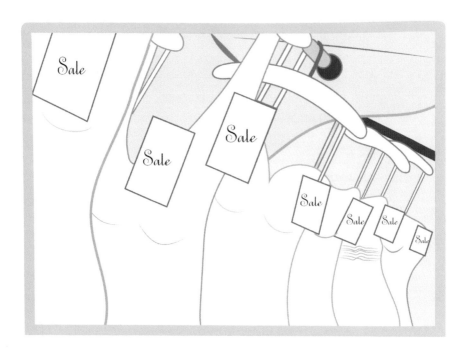

Sample Sale Or To Order New

Every bridal retailer will have a range of dresses for you to try. When you find the one then a new one is made to order specifically for you. To have this option you would pay the full retail price, however, sometimes you may be able to take the dress sample off the shop floor for half the price or less! The only difference is that the dress has been tried on by other brides and may need slight repairs and a dry clean before the wedding day.

Around 2 to 3 times a year a bridal boutique will announce a sale so if you are happy to have a dress that has been a shop sample and get a good deal then keep a look out for sale announcements.

Alternatively, if you were torn between another dress you could always see if the sample has gone in the sale and get to have 2 dresses for the big day! Now wouldn't that be a dream come true and lucky you if you can have this option available to you!

Bridesmaids

Bridesmaids

I would strongly advise choosing your bridesmaid dresses after you have decided on the dress you will be wearing. This is because there is a high chance you may choose a bridal dress you never envisioned on having.

Choosing your dress should be about you and what you love when putting the dress on rather than trying to match the bridesmaid dresses you have already bought.

Bridal dress shopping can be very emotionally tiring so spending your appointment just focused on bridal dresses will be so much easier for you and your bridesmaids. Once you have found the perfect dress and given the biggest item off your list a huge tick and of course to celebrate. The next step would be to arrange a bridesmaid appointment on a separate day. Many boutiques will happily let you put your dress on that you bought with them and have your girls try on bridesmaid dresses and see which dress is best suited with yours.

Wedding planning really does fly by so enjoy the moment and book separate appointments for you and your girls. Lovely memories to share and you get to spend more time together.

Taking pictures

Taking Pictures

*B*efore you take pictures during your bridal appointment double check that the store you are in allow it. In the modern world we live in many boutiques do allow photos and videos to be taken and this can really help with deciding which dress to choose if stuck between a few.

I would advise taking pictures only of the dresses that you like and of dresses that fit you nicely as you can still envision what the dress would be like on the wedding day. The person responsible for taking photos must stand up when taking the picture as it will produce a better image of you than sitting down and pointing upwards.

Most importantly do not let anyone else see the photos that are not meant to. Put them in a secure folder or delete them once no longer needed.

Majority of bridal retailers only allow 2 – 4 guests to accompany you to your appointment. Therefore you could set up a group on your phone to include those who can not attend or better still allow them to video call during your appointment.

Make a day of it

Make A Day Of It

*T*here is a very high chance you will find your dress on your first day of shopping so be prepared and start early ☺

Bridal boutiques normally open at 9am on weekends and 10am in the week. Appointments can last for 1 – 2 hours so you could book between 2 - 4 shops in the day, depending how busy you want to be, with lunch in between and dinner/celebrations afterwards.

If travelling by car, would advise parking in the centre of where the bridal boutiques are located and either taking a taxi or public transport, so you do not have to worry about parking and can enjoy drinks if offered during your appointments.

I have heard of brides booking hotels for the night, so they can enjoy a full day with their entourage, really making the whole wedding dress experience that extra special.

Get dressed up, do your hair the way you envision it to be for the big day, be open when you come to choose dresses to try on and most importantly enjoy every minute. Be prepared to say yes to the dress!!

Saying YES to the dress

Saying Yes To The Dress

The question that is always asked is how will I know the dress is the one? Every bride is different and so no one reacts the same. A dress may make you burst in to tears or laugh with excitement! Another bride may not show any emotion but 100% know the dress she has on is hers. Sometimes your guests will cry other times no tear is shed. It does not mean the dress is not the one we just all react differently in the moment.

When you have "the one" on you can envision it on the day, you can see how your partner will react when he/she sees you for the first time, your entourage are just as excited/emotional to see you in the dress and most importantly you do not want to take it off! Yes you have found the one and getting married has just become real…..again!

Once you have said YES the majority of bridal retailers will give you and your entourage drinks. The start of the celebrations together. When you are ready they just need to take your bust, waist and hip measurement as well as checking your hollow to hem.

Once this is done an order from is filled in and sizes discussed together. When your size has been confirmed and you are happy with everything stated on your order form a 50% deposit is then required to secure your dress. The remaining 50% will be paid when your dress arrives 3 – 9 months later. Pictures are then normally taken of you with your entourage, usually holding a sign saying you said YES ! Lovely memories to have together and reinforces that you have found the one today!

Your dress has now been ordered, celebrations begin and a big tick off your wedding list has been completed. Time is about to speed up for you as you excitedly wait to try your dress on again. Other parts of your wedding planning will now take focus until then. Enjoy every second of it.

Time to stop

Time To Stop

The dress has been chosen and order has been placed. All your focus should now switch to other parts of the wedding planning still to complete. Majority of which will revolve around your bridal dress.

Do not keep looking at pictures of different bridal dresses, they all look beautiful in the photos and doing this constantly and booking bridal appointments to see them could go on forever.

Sometimes it helps to delete all bridal pictures off your phone including the one you chose and to unfollow social media pages that constantly pop up with amazingly staged pictures of dresses on your newsfeeds.

You have found your dress, it is perfect for you and your wedding. Remember how it felt when you had it on, the reaction from your bridal party that were with you and use this to focus on the huge wedding list you still have to complete.

Doing this will make the wedding planning after finding your dress a little bit easier and the excitement to try your dress on again will help speed up time until it has arrived.

When you receive that email or phone call informing you your dress is finally here ! Be prepared for it to feel like Christmas day and to also feel like you are about to take an important exam. This is completely normal as emotions are all over the place until you get to your final appointment to try it on.

When you finally get your dress on it really is the most wonderful feeling as you have waited so long and now it is here and it is yours. Majority of the time it is even better than you would have remembered it. It will confirm again that this is really happening and you are getting married very soon. Enjoy the moment.

Covid - 19

Covid-19

*A*s I am writing this in 2020, Covid-19 has currently changed the world. Many industries have been affected and the wedding industry is one of them. The above information will help wedding dress shopping that little bit easier, however in a pandemic like this there will be a few changes. Expect only one guest to accompany you to your appointment. Allowing other guests to attend your appointment via video call.

Your bridal consultant will not be helping you in and out of dresses but rather letting you step in and out yourself or have your guest help you. They will be there to guide you through your appointment just not as hands on as before.

Going to 3 – 4 shops in one day may not be possible and may not be something you want to do at this time. Do you research, as said previously, about the boutiques you want to visit. Many will do virtual appointments or have a lengthy discussion before hand about your perfect dress so they will have the dresses you need to have on up and ready on the rail before you arrive at the door.

Prepare to make a decision that day so only start trying on dresses when you are seriously looking. There may be a waiting list for second appointments as a result of shops only seeing a handful of appointments a day and making sure a regimental clean is done before and after every appointment seen.

Expect shops to be booked up 4 – 5 weeks in advance, possibly longer. Ordering a dress is still advised a year before the wedding date. The earlier you order the better. This give plenty of time for it to be made and delivered to store.

A bride will still get her dress and her wedding day will happen. It is so upsetting to know thousands of brides weddings have been postponed to 2021 or even 2022. But remember a date can be moved but the memories you will make with your friends and family will last a life time.

Love is not cancelled.

ABOUT THE AUTHOR

E.E DOROTHY

She has worked in the bridal industry for over a decade. Has an award winning bridal business that is well established and constantly dominates the bridal sector. Enjoys helping brides find their perfect dress and creating that memorable experience. Also a busy mum to two girls, when not working all her free time is spent with her family or planning the next venture.

Printed in Great Britain
by Amazon